To Dad, with love —T.R.

The editors would like to thank
BARBARA KIEFER, Ph.D.,
Charlotte S. Huck Professor of Children's Literature,
The Ohio State University, and
JON C. CAMPBELL,
U.S. Geological Survey,
for their assistance in the preparation of this book.

Visit us on the Web!
www.randomhouse.com/kids
Seussville.com

Educators and librarians, for a variety of teaching tools, visit us at
www.randomhouse.com/teachers

Library of Congress Cataloging-in-Publication Data
Rabe, Tish.
There's a map on my lap! : all about maps / by Tish Rabe ; illustrated by Aristides Ruiz.
Includes index. p. cm. — (The Cat in the Hat's learning library)
Summary: The Cat in the Hat teaches Dick and Sally about cartography and the uses of different
kinds of maps.
ISBN 978-0-375-81099-2 (trade) — ISBN 978-0-375-91099-9 (lib. bdg.)
1. Cartography—Juvenile literature. 2. Maps—Juvenile literature. [1. Cartography. 2. Maps.]
I. Ruiz, Aristides, ill. II. Title. III. Series.
GA105.6 .R33 2002 912—dc21 2001048336

Printed in the United States of America
29 28 27 26 25 24 23

Random House Children's Books supports the First Amendment and celebrates the right to read.

There's a Map on My Lap!

by Tish Rabe

illustrated by Aristides Ruiz

The Cat in the Hat's Learning Library®

Random House 🏠 New York

I'm the Cat in the Hat
and I'm happy to say
there's a map on my lap—
let's get on our way!

We will travel the world.
See the whole U.S.A.
And still be back home
by the end of the day!

Maps are drawings that help
to find out where you are
and get where you're going—
no matter how far.

When mapmakers make maps,
they must first decide who
will be using the map
and what it needs to do.

Cartographer

Car-tog-ra-pher is just
a more formal name
for a mapmaker, but
both their jobs are the same.

The map of the earth
that we use most of all
is a globe. Like the earth,
it is round as a ball.

Peel the skin off an orange
and lay it out flat.
A flat map of the earth
would look something like that.

LONGITUDE:

These are lon-gi-tude lines,
which run up and run down.

MERIDIAN
60° 30° 0° 30° 60°
W W E E
PRIME

LATITUDE:

Lat-i-tude lines
go around and around.

90°
60°N
30°N
EQUATOR 0°
30°S
60°S

Now, if maps were the size
of the places they show,
mapmakers would run
out of paper, and so . . .

A chart called a scale
makes maps easy to use,
shrinking miles into inches
on each map that you choose.

SCALE: 1 inch = 100 miles
0   100   200   300   400

SCALE

Makes everything smaller
and helps you and me
carry the world
around easily!

You can make a map of
far places you roam,
or a map—called a plan—
of your very own home.

We used this scale—
one inch equals three feet.
It helped us do something
we both think is neat!
We drew our whole room
so it fits on . . .

0   3FT

1 inch = 3 feet

. . . one sheet!

bedroom
←— 9 ft —→
12 ft
CLOSET

There are four main directions.
All maps have got 'em.
North is on top.
South down at the bottom.

If you look to the right,
that is where East will be.
Look to the left—
and it's West that you see.

West

North

East

South

Compass Rose

To remember all four,
here is one easy way:

"Never Eat Soggy Wheat!"

orth   ast   outh   est

is what I always say.

I have here an atlas.
Come on, take a look!
You will find lots of maps
and they're all in this book.

18

Sometimes maps use pictures
to show where things are.
A capital city is
marked with a star.

A tent shows a campsite.
Tracks show where a train is.
To get to the airport,
just find where a plane is.

LEGEND

☆ CAPITAL CITY

╫ TRAIN

✈ AIRPORT

⛺ CAMPSITE

A chart called a legend,
if you look carefully,
will list and explain
each picture you see.

Some maps use colors
to tell you a lot.

I used blue where it's cold
and red where it's hot.

I made deserts light brown
and jungles bright green.

DESERT
of
DRIZE

JUNGLE
of
NOOL

LEGEND
= DESERT
= JUNGLE

The legend will show you
what these colors mean.

Marine charts help boaters.
These maps let them know
if a rock, reef, or sandbar
is hiding below.

When you visit a city
where you've never been,
a city map helps you
know where to begin.

Here is a map
we both carry around.
It shows where the subway
runs under the ground!

Top-o-graph-i-cal maps
are the kind hikers like.
They use them to choose
which direction to hike.

They show where the land
rises hilly and steep
or goes down into valleys
all rocky and deep.

It's a big world we live in.
Here's one way to hold it.
Pick up a map and then simply—
unfold it!

Dot maps, like this one,
are covered with dots.
Some have a few dots,
but some others have lots.

Each dot stands for something.
On this map you see,
each dot stands for one
Frizzle-Frazzled Frazee.
(Most Frazees live up north,
where the haircuts are free.)

When you look at a map,
it's important to see
there is more than one way
from point A to point B.

Firefighters use maps
when they go fight a fire.
The short way would take them
down Voogel to Vyer.

But traffic on Vyer
can be a disaster.

28

So they choose a long way
that's also much faster.

When you want to go
from Fazode to Fazend,
you can measure the miles,
for the road does not bend.

But in order to go
from Fazode to Fahzing
on the fifteenth of May for the
big Fahzing Sing—

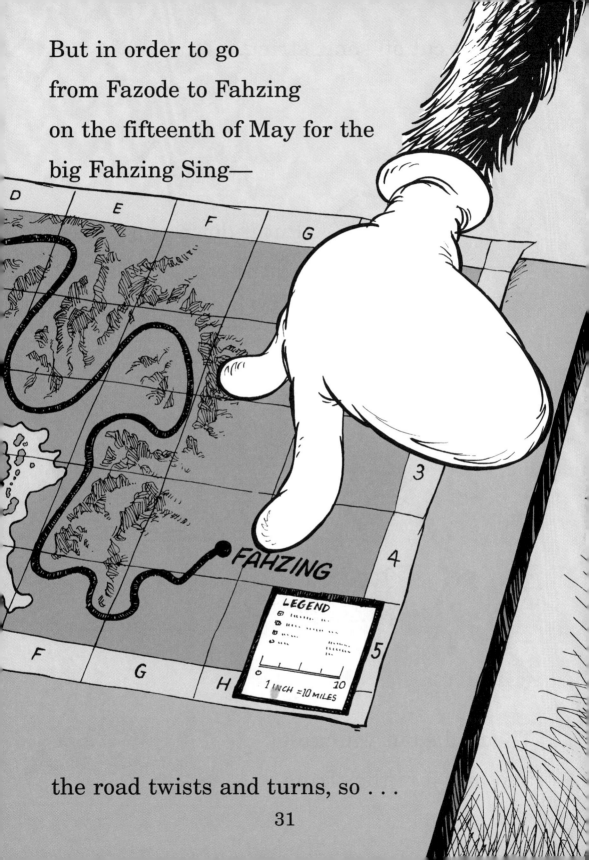

the road twists and turns, so . . .

. . . first cut off some string.

Put it down on the road
all the way to Fahzing.

Then take out your ruler
and measure the string.

The scale on this map
helps you see that it's far.
One inch equals ten miles, so . . .

O 10
ONE INCH = 10 MILES

. . . you should take the car!

WELCOME TO
THE BIG
FAHZING SING

FAHZING

Use this trick to read maps.
You'll be glad that you did.
Some are covered with lines.
This is known as a grid.

There are letters on top.
Numbers run down the side.
Want to find where you are?
Let the grid be your guide.

Trace a line down from A.

Look across at line four.

The lines cross at A4—

at your very own door!

We are having a party.
We're waiting for you.
Take a look at the grid.
There's our house at E2.

Here is a map
that I just got today.
It's a puzzle map
showing the whole U.S.A.

Puzzle maps come in pieces,
and here's the best part—
you can put them together,
then take them apart.

PUZZLE MAP *of the* U.S.A.

INCLUDES ALASKA and HAWAII

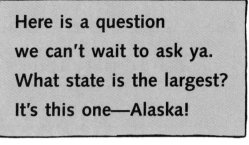

Here is a question
we can't wait to ask ya.
What state is the largest?
It's this one—Alaska!

ALASKA

Now, which of the states
do you think is the smallest?
You're right! It's Rhode Island—
the smallest of all-est!

Here's a game that we play,
so feel free to play too.

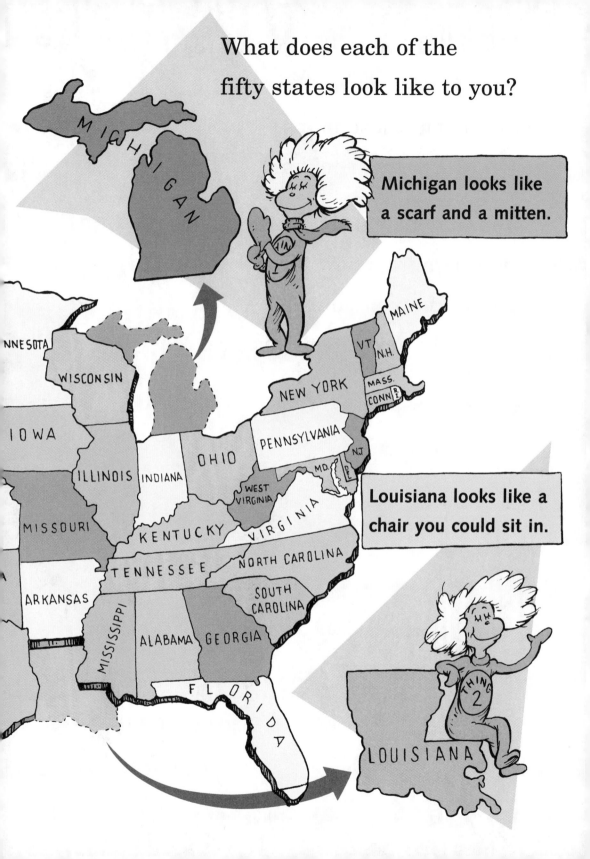

What does each of the
fifty states look like to you?

Michigan looks like
a scarf and a mitten.

Louisiana looks like a
chair you could sit in.

You will have great adventures
your whole life, and so
I give you these maps.
Oh, the places you'll go!

You may travel the world,
but no matter how far,
with a map on your lap
you will know where you are.

You can always use maps.
They will help you in knowing
where you have been
and just where . . .

. . . you are going!

GLOSSARY

Capital: A city where the government of a state or country is located.

Cartographer: A person who makes maps.

Equator: An imaginary line that circles the middle of the earth between the North and South Poles.

Globe: A representation of the earth in the shape of a ball.

Grid: A pattern of lines on a map usually running north-south and east-west that is used for giving positions.

Latitude: Imaginary lines on the earth that run east and west, parallel to the equator.

Legend: The part of a map that lists and explains the symbols, colors, and scale used for the map.

Longitude: Imaginary lines on the earth that run north and south and meet at the poles.

Map: A flat representation of the earth or a part of the earth that shows the relative position of places.

Scale: The relationship between the actual size of an area and its size on a map.

Symbol: A sign or drawing that stands for something else.

Topographical map: A map that shows the shape and changing elevation of the land's surface.

FOR FURTHER READING

Looking at Maps and Globes by Carmen Bredeson (Children's Press, *Rookie Read-About Geography*). Information on how to read maps and globes. For preschoolers and up.

Mapping Penny's World by Loreen Leedy (Henry Holt). After learning about maps in school, Lisa maps all of the favorite places of her dog, Penny. For preschoolers and up.

Maps and Globes by Jack Knowlton, illustrated by Harriett Barton (HarperTrophy). An introduction to the many different kinds of maps and how to read them. For grades 2 and up.

Me on the Map by Joan Sweeney, illustrated by Annette Cable (Dragonfly Books). A girl describes herself and her surroundings with maps of her room, house, street, town, state, and so on. For kindergarten and up.

Our World (National Geographic Society). A first picture atlas for children. For preschoolers and up.

INDEX

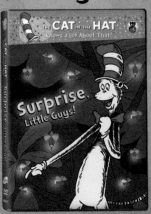